Bygone PETERHEAD

by

Jim Buchan

In addition to boats for the local fishery, at least 100 other vessels, ranging from 30 to 434 tons, were launched from local yards between 1851 and 1885. Some were used as coasters; others plied their trade in the Indian Ocean, the China Sea, and the Antipodes; several became whalers; and a few ranged the Seven Seas wherever cargoes dictated. The *Ariel*, shown here at the West Pier of the South Harbour, was 86 tons, 74 feet long, 20 broad, and 9½ deep. Stephen and Forbes, one of three big shipbuilding firms in the town, launched her in March 1870 from a yard in Bridge Street. Built for the coasting and Baltic trades and designed for speed, she sailed from Peterhead to Stettin, Poland, in considerably less than four days. In 1879 she was sold to a Welsh owner for £500, and became a total loss in November 1904 after running aground at Bearhaven, Ireland, when bound for Swansea with a cargo of copper ore.

© Jim Buchan 1999
First published in the United Kingdom, 1999,
by Stenlake Publishing, 54-58 Mill Square,
Catrine, Ayrshire, KA5 6RD
www.stenlake.co.uk

ISBN 9781840330816

Printed by: Blissetts, Roslin Road, Acton, W3 8DH

ACKNOWLEDGEMENTS

I wish to acknowledge the co-operation I have received from many people – too numerous for all to be named here – when compiling this book. Members of the staff in the public library and in the Arbuthnot Museum, Peterhead, have been very helpful. I especially wish to thank Dr David Bertie, Curator of Local History, Aberdeenshire Council, and Rex Findlay, Museums Photographer, Aberdeenshire Council, for their invaluable assistance.

The publishers would like to thank Nicola Furrie for putting them in touch with the author, and Robert Grieves for supplying the pictures that appear on page 48.

Most of the photographs in this book are from the collection in the Arbuthnot Museum, and have been reproduced with the permission of Aberdeenshire Council. Copies may be purchased from the Arbuthnot Museum, St Peter Street, Peterhead, AB42 1QD.

This book has been published in association with Aberdeenshire Council.

Peter Buchan, Peterhead's fisherman-poet, writing in the local dialect, fantasised that 'THE Buchan', the progenitor of the Buchan Clan in the area, 'wis the mate on Noah's Ark'. He 'girned' so much that 'Noah shivved him ower the side'. Buchan, however, 'wis ower coorse tae droon' and 'swam aboot for fourteen days before he landed sair forfochen at a place ca'd Almanythie'! More seriously, a respected local historian concluded that this 'old Norse landing-place among the Almanythie rocks', albeit 'a mere channel cut through the rocks, with a rough attempt at a wharf', was 'the town's first rude harbour'. When Asiatic cholera appeared in Britain in 1865, seamen on incoming vessels were excluded from Peterhead harbour if they were suspected of being infected. They were rowed ashore at Almanythie Creek and lodged in a two-roomed house in the Roanheads area, with an old fishwife as nurse.

INTRODUCTION

Situated on the coast about 33 miles north-east of Aberdeen, Peterhead is the most easterly town on the mainland of Scotland. The charter creating it a Burgh of Barony on 29 July 1587 empowered George Keith, 5th Earl Marischal, to build a harbour and establish a town at 'Keith Inch alias Peterhead'. (Keith Inch, a rocky peninsula, was linked to the mainland by a wide ridge, the Sand Bridge, passable except at high tide.) The earl built a castle for himself on Keith Inch and constructed a small pier near it; he also built a bulwark at Port Henry. On 1 June 1593 – the same year in which he founded Marischal College, Aberdeen – George Keith granted a feu charter to the original fourteen feu-holders, who were allocated land on which to build houses in 'mainland' Peterhead. His descendants remained Superiors of the town until the Jacobite Earl Marischal was declared forfeit after the failure of the rebellion in 1715. Members of the Edinburgh Merchant Company have been the Superiors since 1728.

About a decade after George Keith granted his feu charter, the local population is estimated to have been in excess of 200. In 1881 there were 10,953 in burghal Peterhead and 3,304 in landward Peterhead; by 1901 the corresponding census returns were 11,794 and 3,352; and by 1931 there were 12,545 in the burgh and 2,740 in the landward area.

Peterhead's prosperity has always been dependent on the availability of harbour facilities appropriate for the maritime activities prevailing at the time. Some of the most eminent civil engineers of their day – Smeaton, Rennie, Telford, and the Stevensons – were employed during the transformation of the primitive harbours into the complex of basins now administered by sixteen Peterhead Harbour Trustees, with powers originally consigned to them by Act of Parliament in 1807. Historically, the trustees have concentrated on the fishing industry – whaling, herring, white fish, mackerel, and shellfish.

After prolonged discussion regarding the establishment of a national Harbour of Refuge, the Government chose Peterhead's South Bay as the most appropriate location and decided to complement the contractors' workforce with convict labour during the construction of the breakwaters.

Peterhead Prison and an adjoining working area, known as the Admiralty Yard, were established. Work began on the south breakwater in the 1890s, and although the north breakwater was not completed until the 1950s, the deep-water anchorage in the bay was used as a naval base in both World Wars. A major service base for the North Sea oil and gas industries has been developed there; a tanker jetty has been built in the south-east corner; and a marina constructed in the south-west corner. Peterhead Bay Harbour Authority, consisting of nine members appointed by the Secretary of State for Scotland, is responsible for operations in the South Bay.

There have always been opportunities for employment in the Peterhead area in industries associated with maritime activities; e.g. ropemaking, sailmaking, ship and boat building, ship repairing, blacksmithing, and fish processing. Another significant source of employment was the granite industry, with over 35,000 tons of the stone being exported between 1817 and 1821. During the latter part of the nineteenth century, Peterhead granite, dressed and polished in the town, was much in demand for the ornamental frontages of prestigious buildings in London and elsewhere, and eight quarries were still being worked in the neighbourhood at the beginning of the twentieth century.

The medicinal properties of the water from the Wynd Well, later known as the Wine Well, were responsible for Peterhead becoming the premier spa in Scotland in the eighteenth century. It is interesting to note that one contributor to a guidebook, eulogising Peterhead as a holiday resort in 1900, drew attention to the chalybeate mineral spring at the Geddle Braes at the northern end of the town. He claimed that it was a neglected asset, the best of its kind in Scotland, and proposed it should be developed and so 'recreate Peterhead as a watering-place'. The town's publicists praised Peterhead's other holiday attractions, especially the golf course and the facilities for cycling. They also highlighted the bracing climate; the wondrously pure air replete with ozone; the therapeutic benefits of baths available near the site of the defunct Wine Well; and the sights and sounds of the summer herring fishing!

George Keith, Earl Marischal, who was empowered by a royal charter to establish 'Keith Inch alias Peterhead' as a Burgh of Barony in 1587, was among the wealthiest nobles in Scotland. One of his many estates was about three miles north-west of Peterhead, at Inverugie, where he is credited with enhancing an old castle by adding 'a splendid double-courtyard Renaissance chateau'. The building is now more ruinous than shown in this photograph (right), which was taken *c.*1890. With her creel and its 'birn' of fish carried free of charge in the guard's van, the fishwife standing near the ruin probably went from Peterhead by railway to a station convenient for her to walk to her regular customers, with whom she bartered her fish for farm produce.

Before the Earl Marischal founded the Burgh of Peterhead, he was in Denmark negotiating a marriage between James VI and the eldest daughter of the Danish king. This did not materialise, but James subsequently married a younger princess, Anne of Denmark. Tradition says that when the earl built his castle on Keith Inch in the 1590s, it was 'after the model of the Palace of the King of Denmark'. In the above 1795 sketch by Montagu Beattie, the tower bears little resemblance to a palace, although it has been suggested that it was a part of a bigger building. In 1780 guns were placed near the castle to guard the South Bay. Before they were removed in 1817 they were fired in anger at least twice – to chase away a notorious privateer and to repel a French vessel. The remains of the earl's castle were demolished in 1813; Castle Street on Keith Inch is the only reminder of its existence.

INVERUGIE CASTLE

A battery of 32 pounders, manned by members of the local Corps of Artillery Volunteers, was deployed on Keith Inch in 1860. When the corps was established in 1859, in response to the Government's appeal for the formation of a national network of coastal defences manned by volunteers, the Secretary of State for War designated it 'the first in Aberdeenshire'. The gunners – some of whom are shown at gun practice, probably in 1860 – displayed a very high standard of marksmanship during the annual inspections of the corps but were never required to man the guns in time of war. The Corps of Artillery Volunteers at Peterhead was amalgamated with other corps to form the 1st Buchan Artillery Volunteers in 1882, a year after the battery on Keith Inch was dismantled.

During the First World War, the 5th Gordon Highlanders were described as being 'Somewhere in France'. This phrase was used to describe the location of all regiments that formed part of the BEF (British Expeditionary Force) on the Western Front, and was presumably introduced as a security measure. The group of 5th Gordon Highlanders shown here posed with a few locals for a souvenir photograph at Amiens in 1916.

After war broke out in August 1914, the 5th Battalion of the Gordon Highlanders mobilised at their depot at Kirk Street, Peterhead – the drill hall which had been built for the Rifle Volunteers in 1880. For the duration of the war, recruits to the battalion received basic training in Peterhead before joining their comrades on the Western Front. Bearing the regimental badge and recording the battalion's battle honours, a granite obelisk was erected near the hall in September 1923 as a memorial to the 5th Gordons. The drill hall was the depot for the 221st (Peterhead) Battery of the Royal Artillery (TA) in the 1930s, but was later demolished to allow road realignments. The memorial and a plaque with the names of members of the 5th Gordons who were killed during the First World War still stand near the site.

Drawn in 1795 by Montagu Beattie, the son of James Beattie, Professor of Moral Philosophy at Marischal College, Aberdeen, this sketch was described as the 'Ruins of an old Roman Catholic chapel near Peterhead with the manse and part of the town from the SW'. A church dedicated to St Peter stood on or near this site at the Kirk Burn by 1132. A new church, also dedicated to St Peter, was built in the mid-thirteenth century. The building was renovated several times but was eventually abandoned in 1770, when materials and fittings salvaged from the ruin were sold for only £20. The long ecclesiastical association with St Peter is said to be responsible for the naming of the town.

Another of Montagu Beattie's sketches drawn in 1795, this view of the town from the south includes the only known illustration of the parish church, with the large window in the gable, which was opened in 1771 to replace the medieval building. With seats for a congregation well in excess of a thousand, it had been erected on sandy soil too near the sea. By 1800, when the minister described it as 'a crazy fabric, with three broken rafters, floor rotten, walls cracked', it had to be abandoned for safety reasons. For the next six years the congregation was allowed to worship in the Episcopalian chapel in Chapel Street until a new Presbyterian parish church was built.

The ruins of the medieval parish church, viewed here from the seaward side, had been sketched a century earlier by Montagu Beattie (see previous page). Although Beattie was correct in describing it as 'Ruins of an old Roman Catholic chapel', he omitted to add that from the time of the Scottish Reformation it had been alternately used by the establishment of the day – Presbyterian or Episcopalian. After the church was abandoned in 1770, the churchyard remained a place for burials. The bell-tower survived and is said to have been a convenient watchtower for those on guard against body-snatchers.

The new parish church, costing £3,575 12s., was opened on 1 August 1806. Its spire, 118 feet high and 'in the style of Sir Christopher Wren', is prominent near the top left corner of this photograph, taken *c*.1870. Planned for a congregation of 1,875, the austere appearance of the church is said to have resulted from the fact that the cost of any ornamental features had to be paid by voluntary subscriptions! 'Massive building, Minus beauty, Tempests shielding, Does its duty' was the typically laconic expression of local opinion regarding the architectural and functional merits of the church. With a congregational hall and porch added in 1896, and familiarly known as the Muckle Kirk, it continues to do its duty. The Town House spire is in the middle distance.

FIELD-MARSHAL KEITH Born at Inverugie, 1696. Killed in the Battle of Hochkirchen, 14th October 1758. The gift of King William 1st of Prussia to the Town of Peterhead, 23rd August 1868. Probus vixit. Fortis Obiit. (*Loosely translated*: 'Pure he lived; a hero he died.')

The Town House was erected in 1788, and this 1860 photograph shows it with the granite forestairs that were subsequently removed. It replaced the Tolbooth, where contraband liquor was occasionally hidden under the floor to elude the excisemen when smuggling was rife in Peterhead. The initial cost of the Town House, £2,000, was paid by means of an eighteenth century version of a private finance initiative, with contributions from various public bodies, local inhabitants, the Community of Feuars, and the town's Superiors, the Governors of the Merchant Maiden Hospital, Edinburgh. The Town House was not insured until 1826, when it was covered for only £1,500. At 125 feet high it has the town's tallest spire, which like that of the new parish church has also been described as being 'in the Wren style of architecture'.

This brief epitaph, on the pedestal of the statue, commemorates James Francis Edward Keith, the most renowned native of Buchan. He fled abroad after joining his older brother, the Earl Marischal, in an abortive attempt to start a Jacobite rebellion in 1719. After a distinguished career in Spain, Russia and Prussia as a soldier of fortune and diplomat, he was promoted a Field Marshal and Governor of Berlin, where a marble statue was erected in his memory. When it was moved to the Military Academy, a bronze replica took its place in the Wilhelmsplatz. Another replica was gifted to Peterhead where it was erected, on 16 August 1869, on the site it still occupies in front of the Town House.

Right: By the time this photograph was taken – probably about 1910 – there had been several alterations to the Town House, both internally and externally. In 1881 the frontage was given a face-lift when the forestairs were removed and replaced by a vestibule and flight of concrete steps inside. Rooms in the Town House were occasionally used for unlikely purposes; as an armoury for the volunteers; a fire-station; a soup kitchen; the parish school; the town jail; for meetings of the Reading Society of Peterhead; and as the Mechanics' Library. The Music Hall, with three multi-purpose function rooms as well as anterooms and accommodation for the hall-keepers, is visible beyond the Town House. Its foundation stone was laid with full Masonic honours in July 1872. By the time the construction workers had been entertained to a ball in the lower hall of the new building in October 1873 it had cost over £4,000.

Left: In later years, the lower hall in the Music Hall became the Empress Hall, a popular venue for dancers. One of the other halls was adapted for use as a cinema, later renovated as The Picture House, where, on Saturday 12 December 1936, the audience enjoyed the film *Queen of Hearts* starring Gracie Fields. Next morning, one of the staff in the nearby Northern Hotel (now the Caledonian Hotel) raised the alarm; the Music Hall was on fire. Despite the efforts of local firemen and colleagues from Aberdeen, the building was a smouldering shell by nightfall. There were no fatalities and no serious injuries but extensive damage, estimated at £50-£60,000, was done to neighbouring shops. Electricity supplies were disrupted when the adjacent Peterhead Electricity Company's showroom and transformer station were also gutted. The 'Kirkin' of the Council', in the old parish church, was postponed because the Provost and his colleagues were at the scene of the disaster.

The local Whigs commemorated the passing of the Parliamentary Reform Bill in 1832 by building the Meethill Tower, now surrounded by houses, on the southern outskirts of the town. The Tories riposted by erecting the Reform Monument on the site of the old market cross in Broad Street in 1833. Shown here surrounded by an iron railing, probably in the 1870s or 1880s, the granite pillar is surmounted by a rampant lion above a plaque bearing the Earl Marischal's arms. The plaque was originally on the gateway at Inverugie Castle. A Latin inscription on the monument translates as, 'Small resources are increased by concord; wealth vanishes by discord'. The gun in the foreground of the photograph, situated at the east end of Broad Street, was one of those which, captured from the Russians at Sebastopol during the Crimean War, were later put on permanent display in various towns in the British Isles. This one was subsequently moved to Bath Street, where it remained until it was melted down for the war effort during the Second World War.

Montagu Beattie drew the sketches reproduced on pages 4, 7, and 45 when on holiday in Peterhead with his father, Professor James Beattie. The latter was one of the many visitors who came regularly to 'take the waters' from the mineral spring when the town was in its heyday as a spa. Another habitué was the Duchess of Gordon, who secured her place in the folklore of the North-east by the part she played in a recruiting campaign when her son was raising the regiment which became known as the Gordon Highlanders; she rewarded those who enlisted with a kiss! This photograph of the foreshore near the entrance to the South Harbour was taken about a century after the Beatties visited Peterhead. The well-house is the small building behind the vessel's boom. On the left is the Masonic Lodge and, across from it, part of the New Inn is visible on what is now the corner of Jamaica Street and Lodge Walk.

Named St Peter's Well when it was discovered in the 1590s, the mineral spring's medicinal properties were later promoted as a veritable panacea for ills of every description by Dr Andrew More. A native of Peterhead, he was Professor of Physic (i.e. medicine) at King's College, Aberdeen, from 1642 to 1680. Several analysts emphasised the iron content of the spring; one even claimed that 'because the waters of it run on iron and vitriol, it is reckoned to have all the virtues of steel'! It was later known as the Wine Well, allegedly a corruption of Wynd Well, the name given to it because of its proximity to the Wynd, now James Street. The well-house, with the Keith arms above the door, is said to have been erected in 1775. When it was demolished in the 1930s the stone bearing the Keith arms was built into a wall to commemorate its place in the history of Peterhead.

In 1759 the Freemasons built Keith Lodge beside the Wine Well; the top of the well-house can be seen above the railing on the left. The Masons extended the Lodge in the 1770s and, for the convenience of visitors, fitted up two bathing-rooms and a pump-room, with a serving-woman in attendance. Admission to the pump-room cost a crown for the season; one guinea was charged for a season's use of the baths. The drawing-room in the Lodge was available for use as a tea-room or ballroom when required. Soon afterwards, the New Inn was built nearby with seven public rooms, twenty-two bedrooms, and a well-appointed dining-room. The proprietor's miniature zoo was an extra attraction for visitors, as were displays of acrobatics, tightrope walking, dancing, and horsemanship by travelling artistes. No trace of the New Inn remains. The Masonic Lodge, demolished in 1937, is commemorated in the name Lodge Walk and by a memorial plaque inserted by the Freemasons in a wall there.

Bath Street, a continuation of Lodge Walk, shown at its junction with Merchant Street. Its name is reminiscent of the outdoor bathing pool which James Arbuthnot, a local druggist, cut from the solid rock in 1800. Located so that the bathers were 'properly defended from the view', it measured 90 feet by 30 and had a sluice to control the depth of the sea-water which flowed into it every flood tide. Two years later, to diversify the curative regimen of those taking the waters, he built suites of warm baths so that 'patients may be accommodated with the steam or vapour, hot air, projecting and shower baths, at any degree of temperature which may be required'. Soon afterwards, when the Wine Well slowed to a trickle and there were signs of pollution, Peterhead's popularity as a spa declined. The baths became ruinous and only the outdoor pool remained usable. In 1898 the town council cleared the site and built an indoor swimming pool, which was used until the pool adjoining the Community Centre was opened in 1978.

GREAT NORTH OF SCOTLAND GRANITE Co.
LIMITED.

EDINBURGH INTERNATIONAL EXHIBITION
1886
ONLY GOLD MEDAL

PHILADELPHIA EXHIBITION 1878
PRIZE MEDAL

PETERHEAD, SCOTLAND.

WILLIAM MARTIN, MANAGER,

RED GRANITE,

OF RICHEST COLOUR AND FINEST QUALITY
FOR MONUMENTAL AND ARCHITECTURAL PURPOSES
DESIGNS AND ESTIMATES ON APPLICATION.

WORKS—ADJOINING RAILWAY STATION.   QUARRIES—BLACKHILL.

Quarries in the Peterhead area – of which there were about twenty in the nineteenth century, but only one by the 1950s – produced the best weathering red granite. Large quantities of hewn stone, the traditional local building material, were exported from the 1790s onwards. Thomas Telford pronounced the granite 'very proper for wharfs, piers of harbours and bridges, and for forming tide walls' and John Rennie came specially to Peterhead to acquire big blocks when he was building Southwark Bridge. Peterhead granite was also in demand for monumental purposes and for ornamental frontages for public buildings. About 1861, when it was said there were only three granite-polishing works in the world, stone-polishing began at Invernettie, where the Score (Europe) engineering works now stand. From 1871 until 1916, on a site now occupied by Peterhead Academy, granite polishing was carried on by the Great North of Scotland Granite Company. Their high quality work was incorporated in many prestigious buildings, e.g. the Stock Exchange, Covent Garden, the Foreign Office, and Australia House in London.

In 1886 an Act of Parliament authorised the establishment of a Harbour of Refuge in the South Bay, Peterhead. The bay was chosen because of its depth of water; its strategic position for shipping in the North Sea; and the proximity of an abundant supply of granite. Before the construction of the breakwaters could begin, several ancillary projects had to be undertaken. Scotland's only penal prison was built to house the convicts who were to be part of the workforce. Stores for sand, cement, and coal; facilities for mixing concrete and casting the building blocks; sheds for carpentry, smithing, and stone dressing; and an array of railway sidings were built in the Admiralty Yard, an area adjoining the prison. A standard-gauge railway was constructed to link the yard with the barge harbour, the south breakwater, and the granite quarry at Stirling Hill. This photograph, taken in 1905, shows Peterhead Prison with the Admiralty Yard beyond it on the right. The partially-completed south breakwater, with a Titan crane at work, is visible to the left.

The construction of railway links from the Admiralty Yard and the south breakwater to Stirling Hill quarry – about two-and-a-half miles to the south – involved the building of six bridges, one of which was a five-arched viaduct. Officially known as the British State Railway, because it was the only state-owned passenger-carrying railway in the country, it was operational by the end of 1889. Prisoners were conveyed between a platform in the Admiralty Yard and the Stirling Hill terminus in four specially built carriages. Prison warders carried cutlasses while, as shown below, guards with rifles were positioned at the quarry. Four engines were available to pull the wagon-loads of granite, extracted by the convicts, to the Admiralty Yard or directly to the barge harbour or south breakwater.

This Titan crane was custom-built in Bath for laying the massive concrete blocks used in building the south breakwater of the Harbour of Refuge. It was delivered to Peterhead railway station in sections, and after being assembled on the construction site was operational early in 1892. One man could control all its movements from the cab, and with its 32 wheels running on rails it was capable of carrying in excess of 60 tons at 24 feet per minute. This picture shows the breakwater at an early stage, with only the pilework for the barge harbour in place. When completed, this small harbour was used by specially adapted barges for the shipment of concrete blocks, rubble boulders, and other materials during the construction of both breakwaters.

On account of lessons learned from damage caused by North Sea storms while it was under construction, and because of Treasury limits on spending, engineers were forced to make amendments to the original specifications of the south breakwater. It was shortened from the planned 3,250 feet to 2,850 feet. The roundhead at the outer end of the breakwater was finished and surmounted by a lighthouse in 1914.

By 1922 the north breakwater – planned to be 1,500 feet long – was about half finished. The project had already cost more than £900,000 and was well over-budget. This was at the time of the infamous 'Geddes Axe', when public expenditure was being closely scrutinised and a policy of widespread cost-cutting was introduced. Severe financial constraints thereafter meant that work on the breakwater progressed slowly. The Second World War caused a further interruption and it was not until 27 September 1956 that some of the employees, including several divers, posed for a commemorative photograph on the completion of the Harbour of Refuge project. Queen Victoria was still on the throne when work had begun!

No trace remains of the Invernettie Brickwork, which stood near the shore of the South Bay on a site now partly occupied by the Maritime Heritage building. In 1900 a guidebook mentioned the lane, 'formerly used in connection with the brickwork', which passed the former owner's cottage on the way to the beach. Many of the 250,000 bricks and tiles said to have been produced annually in the early years of the nineteenth century were shipped from the brickwork's own 'tidy little harbour'. Pipes for Fraserburgh's water supply were made here, and it has been claimed that Peterhead pantiles were as good as those made in Holland! An erstwhile owner, James Forbes, emigrated to America and became well-known as a portrait painter in Chicago, where many of his best paintings were destroyed in the Great Fire in 1871. Before emigrating he gave lessons to aspiring artists. His most famous pupil was John Philip, later known as the 'Scottish Velasquez' or 'Spanish John'.

During the 1840s and 50s, Peterhead was the main port in the country for Arctic whalers. In addition to vessels launched from local yards or in various British east coast ports, boats built in Prussia, Nova Scotia, and New Brunswick were included in Peterhead's 'Greenland Fleet'. The number of vessels engaged in hunting seals and whales peaked at thirty-one in 1857, declining steadily thereafter; thirteen whalers sailed from the port in 1865. In spite of the downturn in the industry, members of the town's leading whaling family – the Grays – contracted with A. Hall and Co., Aberdeen, for two purpose-built, steam-powered vessels; the *Eclipse* in 1867 and the *Hope*, shown here, in 1873. Arthur Conan Doyle, a medical student at Edinburgh University and later the creator of Sherlock Holmes, sailed for a season as surgeon on the *Hope*. In 1882 she was chartered for the rescue of members of Leigh Smith's expedition after their vessel – the Peterhead-built screw steam yacht *Eira* – was wrecked in Franz Josef Land.

Seen here at Scott's Pier in her home port, the *Windward* was the last whaler to be built in Peterhead. With timbers of oak, teak and greenheart, and a wooden hull reinforced with iron plates at the bows, she had a gross tonnage of 321 when launched in 1860. Six years later she was the first Peterhead-built vessel to have steam engines installed. The *Windward*'s last voyage as a whaler, in 1893, signalled the end of the local whaling industry. After being sold furth of Peterhead, she was used in an expedition to Franz Josef Land in 1896 and was involved in the rescue of Fridtjof Nansen, the Norwegian explorer. She was also used in Richard Peary's attempts to reach the North Pole before being lost in Smith's Sound in 1907.

When the Earl Marischal built his castle on Keith Inch (page 4), he had difficulty in finding a good source of drinking water until a well was sunk on the east side of what is now the South Harbour. He employed Andrew Phinnie to oversee the well and carry water to the castle. Phinnie was succeeded as water-carrier by his son, also called Andrew Phinnie, who built a house near the well in the latter part of the seventeenth century. The property was subsequently enlarged and used as a granary. It later became a store – note the herring nets hung out to dry near the entrance – but until its demolition in 1937 was always known as 'Phinnie's House'. Between 1889 and 1909, when she sank in the North Sea, the *Bernadotte*, a Norwegian tramp steamer, was a frequent visitor to the South Harbour during the herring season.

'Mainland' Peterhead was originally linked with Keith Inch by a tidal ridge known as the Sand Bridge. In the 1730s stones cleared from the South Harbour were used to build a causeway across the ridge and so provide round-the-clock access to Keith Inch. This made passage between the North and South Harbours impossible, and vessels could be wind bound in one while the other remained open. This problem was solved in 1850 when the Junction Canal was cut to link the harbours (although the new canal caused tidal swell in the inner basins and booms had to be used to counter this). A swing-bridge, designed by David Stevenson – uncle of the author, Robert Louis Stevenson – was built across the canal. Tested for 9 tons, the bridge was said to be able to carry twice as much and was strong enough to support the carts loaded with huge granite blocks which were exported from local quarries. Although it expanded so much in the summer heat in 1864 that it could not be opened, the bridge was obviously built to last, and was not replaced until the 1950s.

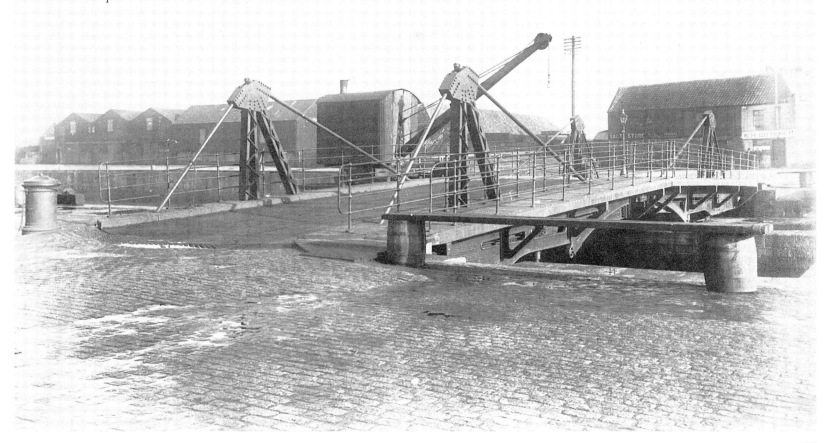

This photograph of the area of the North Harbour known as 'Lazy Hole' shows work on the deepening of Port Henry basin, beyond the far jetty, in full swing. Work began there in 1896 and was completed in time for the harbour to be reopened on 22 June 1897, coinciding with celebrations for Queen Victoria's Diamond Jubilee. During the reconstruction of Port Henry, two of the vessels in the photograph were simultaneously in Peterhead on two occasions. The Leith-registered *Pomona,* the biggest vessel in the basin, was wind bound for three days in September 1896, when the *Industry* (of Findochty), berthed astern of the *Pomona*, was also in the harbour. On 9 February 1897 the *Industry* arrived from Sunderland with a cargo of coal and sailed for Granton on 3 March; the *Pomona* arrived with a load of staves for making barrels on 20 February and left for Bo'ness on 6 March.

The deepening of the South Harbour, shown here nearing completion, was the last phase in a programme of harbour improvements which began in the 1890s. Port Henry and the North and South Harbours were developed into a complex of basins more suitable for the increasing number of steam drifters using the port – large areas had 12 feet below low water at spring tides. Debris from the work, including an estimated 70,000 cubic yards of rock and silt from the South Harbour, was deposited on the foreshore opposite Bath Street and Charlotte Street to make the Smith Embankment. Named in honour of Provost John Smith, it reclaimed about 8 acres. To the right of the coffer-dam is the fish market, which was built on the West Pier of the South Harbour between 1898 and 1900. It was eventually demolished after being replaced by a much bigger market on Greenhill.

Work on deepening the South Harbour was completed in May 1908. According to one contemporary report, about 9,000 spectators watched workmen playing football on the harbour floor and 3,000 children posed for a souvenir photograph before Provost William Leask opened the sluice to flood the basin.

On 24 June 1908 the Master of the Edinburgh Merchant Company, representing the town's Superiors, and Provost Leask sailed from the North Harbour, via the South Bay, to the South Harbour, where they jointly performed the reopening ceremony by cutting the ribbon across the entrance. The town's economy was expected to profit from the improvements to the port, but residents in the harbour area had more personal reasons for welcoming the end of the engineering works. Inhabitants of houses near the quays could sleep free of the noise of a nightshift working in the glare of electric lighting from a dynamo driven by a gas engine. There were no more interruptions due to the underwater blasting of solid rock and traffic around the piers and jetties moved more freely with the dismantling of the 'street railway', which had been used to transport the debris to the Smith Embankment.

In 1919 Peterhead Harbour Trustees discussed an ambitious series of harbour improvements. Little was done until £78,000 was earmarked for a radically modified programme which began in September 1930. Port Henry Harbour was deepened; the Model Jetty was widened; Birnie's Pier was strengthened; Elliot's Jetty was demolished to allow better access; and in July 1932 a new patent slipway was opened by the former Scottish Secretary, William Adamson. A Glasgow firm fitted all the slipway appliances – cradles, travelling gear, hoisting machinery, and an electrically operated lifting-bridge. Firms from Aberdeen and Edinburgh carried out the ancillary work, and so great emphasis was placed on the fact that the project was 'an all Scottish concern'. The importance of this investment in providing proper facilities for the repair and maintenance of the local fishing fleet is illustrated in this photograph of PD147, the *Fertility*; PD99, the *Roseacre*; and PD72, the *Egbert*, pulled high and dry from the harbour and sitting securely in the travelling cradles of the recently installed slipway.

This building, facing Charlotte Street, was erected in 1858 by the United Presbyterians, a denomination formed by the union in 1820 of two sects – Burghers and Anti-burghers – who had previously seceded from the Church of Scotland. It replaced a church which stood on almost the same site, but faced Uphill Lane and so was known locally as the Brae Kirk. The United Presbyterians and the Free Church of Scotland amalgamated as the United Free Church of Scotland in 1900. After the minister of the church on Charlotte Street retired in 1917, the congregation moved to the United Free Church on St Peter Street. Thereafter the building on Charlotte Street was used as a Naval club; an ex-Service Men's Club; and the local institute of the Royal National Mission to Deep Sea Fishermen. It was subsequently demolished during a house-building programme in the area.

In a scene typical of the late summer in the 1880s and 90s, before the era of steam-powered drifters, the herring fleet leaves port bound for the area off the Buchan coast where fish from the Norwegian Deep annually came to spawn. During the season, several hundred 'stranger' drifters – from ports such as Wick, Lossiemouth, Buckie, Banff, and Kirkcaldy – made Peterhead their temporary base and combined with locally-owned vessels to significantly increase the quantity of herring landed. It has been said that 849 herring boats fished from the port in 1881, an all-time record. The most popular models were the 'Fifie', with bow and stern both perpendicular, and the 'Zulu', with perpendicular bow and raked stern. The former is said to have originated on the southern Fife coast; the latter, combining the Fifie's bow with the stern of an older type, the 'Scaffie', first appeared on the Moray Firth coast during the Zulu War.

A Fraserburgh registered Fifie, probably photographed in the 1890s, being poled into harbour in Peterhead. None of the boats have any kind of shelter on deck for the crew, and the helmsman, at his post near the stern, was completely exposed to the elements. Some of the boats have a tiller, or 'tillie' as it was known locally, to move the rudder for steering; a wheel replaced the tiller on newer vessels. A capstan is visible near the stern of the boat on the extreme right. This was a late Victorian innovation to ease the hard manual labour of hauling in the nets which had been 'shot', i.e. thrown overboard, the previous evening. Corks on the net-rope and inflated canvas buoys kept the nets upright in the water to form a kind of long, meshed wall tied to the boat. By allowing the boat to drift for some hours, the fishermen hoped that a shoal of herrings would swim into the nets before they were hauled. When steam-powered drifters replaced the sailing boats, the capstan was located near the bow to reduce the chance of the propeller at the stern being fouled when the nets were being hauled.

The South Harbour was tightly packed at the height of the herring season, August 1914, when the usual 'strangers' from other ports augmented the locally registered fleet of 196 steam drifters. The future of the fishery, however, was uncertain. Crews were depleted when Naval Reservists, including more than 200 of the 'hired men' who came annually from the Highlands and Islands to find seasonal employment, were mobilised at the start of the First World War. The Admiralty soon requisitioned many drifters to work as fleet auxiliaries or minesweepers. As long as the war lasted, fishermen were unable to keep to their customary seasonal pattern of following the herring from Ireland, via the Minch and the northern isles, to east coast ports in Scotland and then south to Yarmouth and Lowestoft.

After the First World War, fishermen were hopeful of reviving the herring industry. Drifters requisitioned by the Admiralty were returned to their owners and younger fishermen, in keeping with long-established practice, bought shares in vessels being added to the fleet. (Ownership of a drifter was divided into 64 shares, which were held in varying amounts by some of the crew and by shore-based partners, e.g. fish salesmen, coal merchants, and ship chandlers.) The pattern of following the herring according to the season was re-established. 'Strangers' were once again a common sight around the coast; here a Yarmouth registered drifter is leaving the South Harbour. In the 1920s, however, the continental market for cured herrings collapsed. Profit margins fell steadily and the future of the herring industry became increasingly precarious during the Depression in the 1930s. Motor-boats, more economical and more suitable for other kinds of fishing, progressively replaced the steam drifters, the last of which in the local fleet, the *Ocean Raleigh*, made its final trip from the port in 1958.

In the Victorian era, herring curers set up temporary 'stations' on land leased on quays or areas near the harbours. During the 1880s the usual rent was 4½d per square yard for a season's lease. Some permanent 'yards', similar to this one on Greenhill, were established by the bigger curers. They gave 'arles', an advance payment to engage the 'guttin' quines' (women who worked in crews of two gutters and a packer) for the season. They also agreed the amount the quines were to be paid at the end of the season for each barrel they had filled with cured herrings. The herrings, sprinkled with rough salt as they were being unloaded from the drifter, were salted again as they were emptied into large movable wooden troughs called 'farlans'. Working at lightning speed with a short-bladed knife known as a 'futtle', the gutters removed the guts and threw the herrings into the 'selection' tubs, according to the size and condition of the fish. Each selection was then separately packed in barrels, with more salt and brine to effect a satisfactory cure and so gain the 'Crown Brand' stamp as a guarantee of quality.

In order to reduce congestion around the harbour basins, the annual leasing of space for curing-stations on the quays was stopped. Yards were established on several streets where, at first, the traditional *modus operandi* of the old curing stations continued. In later years, however, yards were planned with some attention to work study. The gutters worked under cover at one side of the farlans, which were raised to a more suitable working height. They were usually placed linearly against a wall at conveniently spaced openings, through which they could be filled directly from vehicles in the street. In this old-style yard on Windmill Street, a suited and bowler-hatted curer has joined his workforce of guttin' quines and coopers. The latter supervised operations in the yard to ensure that the cure would gain the Crown Brand; between seasons they were employed in making barrels. The North School, visible at the opposite side of the street, was an integral part of the town's response to the requirements of the 1872 Education Act. Built by the Burgh School Board in 1877 at a cost of £2,500, the school was extended and refurbished several times before being closed in 1981.

The makeshift 'hospital', first used near the creek at Almanythie during the cholera outbreak in the 1860s (see page 2), was demolished in 1879 to make way for fishermen's houses in the Roanheads. In the following year a custom-built hospital – the 'but-and-ben' shown here – was erected in the Ive Park. Commonly known as the Old Fever Hospital, this humble building was demolished in 1933. It had been replaced by a new hospital for patients with infectious diseases long before then.

Provost William Leask laid the foundation stone of a fourteen-bed infectious diseases hospital in Buchanhaven on 17 June 1905. He told the spectators, in typically forthright terms, that interfering national authorities had forced the town council to build the hospital, which had been designed by the Burgh Surveyor. Claiming that the Old Fever Hospital had been under-used, he forecast that the robust good health of the citizens of Peterhead would result in the new facility being surplus to requirements. At an estimated cost of £4,000, it was, in his opinion, a total waste of money. When the hospital was completed in April 1907 members of the public were invited to inspect its state-of-the-art furnishings. It subsequently became known as the Ugie Hospital, and with various alterations and additions is still in use.

The Hospital, Peterhead

Soon after the opening of the Ugie Hospital, enteric fever was diagnosed in the town. At the peak of the epidemic in July 1907, 193 cases were identified, and 10 people died. The new hospital could not cope. Arrangements for patients to be admitted to Strichen Hospital proved inadequate, and so a wooden building was erected as a temporary hospital in Peterhead. People were advised to boil all water for at least half an hour and, when Grange Reservoir was emptied for cleaning, a water shortage followed. An emergency water supply was provided from a non-infected source at the Admiralty Yard at the prison. As shown here at 72 King Street, James Sutherland, later a legend in the annals of transport in Buchan (see page 48), was engaged to cart barrels of water for distribution in various parts of the town. By October the epidemic had passed and the town council had made plans to replace the water mains and install new water filtration systems at the reservoirs.

Peterhead's first fire-engine, a 'Mansion House' model with a manually-operated pump, cost £105. In March 1861 it was housed in a makeshift fire-station – the north end of the Town House! A local paper commented that 'It is not over convenient to take a vehicle, with or without springs, up or down a flight of stone steps, especially when such has to be done in a hurry and generally during the darkest hours of the night!' During the first practice session, there was not enough water pressure for its potential to be fully demonstrated. It was used in earnest for the first time on 31 May 1861. A fire was discovered in the Kirkburn Mill at 4.15 p.m., the fire-engine arrived within 15 minutes, and the fire was extinguished by about six o'clock. When no longer serviceable as a fire-engine, its pumping mechanism was removed and, as shown here, it was used to carry coal for the tar boiler belonging to the town council's roads department.

After consulting the Fire-master in Glasgow regarding the merits of various fire-engines, Peterhead Town Council decided, on 4 November 1907, to buy a Merryweather double cylinder 'Greenwich Gem' model. With accessories including 160 yards of best canvas hose, the horse-drawn vehicle cost £328. Its steam-powered engine could pump 400 gallons per minute and could throw 1, 2, or 4 jets simultaneously. It was designed so that the engineer, at his post at the back, could light and stoke the boiler fire for the steam-powered pump while travelling to the scene of the fire.

The incongruous collection of items featured in the windows – guns, smokeless cartridges, Nobel's ammunition, Spanish port, Wild Woodbine cigarettes, locust beans – and the signs advertising tea, cocoa, and chocolate give some indication of the variety of goods on sale in James Cassie's shop. They also illustrate Mr Cassie's idiosyncratic approach to window-dressing. When he died in 1930, at the advanced age of 88, a local paper recalled his famous 'shoppie' at 73 Marischal Street. 'In its day, it was a landmark, an emporium which, if it did not literally contain everything from a needle to an anchor, was replete with most of the commodities needed in an up-to-date community. Its *pièce de résistance* was a display of locust beans. No matter what changes might be made in the process of window display, these were always on view. The only concession Mr. Cassie was ever known to make to the taste for variety was to move the beans, on very rare and special occasions, from one window to the other!' They appear in the right-hand window in this picture.

The inset shows another of the sketches drawn by Montagu Beattie in 1795 and features 'a windmill near Peterhead'. It is said to have been a vaulted tower mill, a type peculiar to Scotland in the seventeenth and eighteenth centuries, and was used for grinding malt and striking pot (pearl) barley. After it stopped working early in the nineteenth century, the sails and wooden windcap, with the mechanism for turning it into the wind, were removed. The tower, shown in the main picture, survived until 1937, when it was demolished to make way for houses. The windmill stood on a site across the road from the football stadium, on what is now Balmoor Terrace, known to older local residents as Windmill Brae.

It is said that golf was introduced to Peterhead in 1841 and was played on the Town Links, near the old Church of St Peter, for the next fifty years. A nine-hole course with a small 'Golf House', was established at Craigewan, on the north side of the River Ugie, in 1892. The original clubhouse burned down in 1896 and the Golf Pavilion – shown here on the day it was opened with due ceremony – was erected in the following year. Costing £203, it was described as 'a spacious and commodious building containing a large front room, a ladies' room, and refreshment room'. The course was claimed to be ideal since 'the uncommon natural advantages of the ground had been fully utilised' and although it was 'perhaps a little too heavy for ladies, the club membership included a number of very good lady players'.

By the time the photograph on the left was taken in the early 1920s, the clubhouse had been extended and a tea-room added. Visitors were informed that, 'only about ten minutes' walk from the railway station', there were two 18-hole courses at Craigewan with 'conditions unrivalled in any east-coast holiday resort in Scotland'. During the holiday season the daily fees were 2s 6d for men and 2s for ladies and juniors. The corresponding charges for a month were £1 and 15s. Toll-paying passengers crossed the River Ugie by ferry. The boat was linked by a pulley at each end to a cable stretched across the river, enabling the ferryman to utilise the current to propel it from bank to bank.

Alexander Birnie, son of George Birnie, one-time harbourmaster in Peterhead, returned home after amassing a fortune from pearl fishing off the Australian coast and financed the building of a bridge across the River Ugie in memory of his father. The George Birnie Memorial Bridge was opened on 11 April 1925. The clubhouse shown here was eventually abandoned when it was said to be in danger of collapsing because of erosion of the dunes. Its successor, built further inland, has also been replaced, along with the Birnie Bridge.

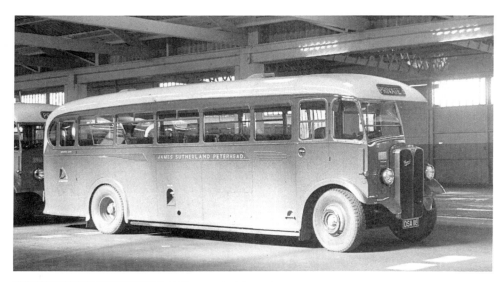

Starting from humble beginnings in the era of the horse and cart, James Sutherland established one of the leading firms in the North-east, incorporating lorries, buses, and farms. When officials from the local railway company approached him with a take-over bid, he is alleged to have asked, 'Foo much will ye tak for yer trainie?' ('How much will you accept for your railway company?'). Sutherland's lorries were especially prominent during the herring fishing seasons in the North-east and East Anglia from the 1920s until the nationalisation of road transport. With its headquarters at the Victoria Stables, Peterhead, and depots in Rosehearty, Cruden Bay, and Methlick, the company's fleet of some eighty vehicles provided most of the bus services in the Buchan area until the Alexander section of the Scottish Bus Group acquired them in 1950. DSA 116, an AEC 'Regal', and the double-deck 'Titan' were among the new vehicles purchased in 1947 to cope with the burgeoning number of bus passengers in the early post-war years.